Second Language Acquis

Starting from the premise that language instruction should be informed by how humans learn language, this module on second language acquisition (SLA) aims to provide teachers at any level with a comprehensive and up-to-date introduction to the key findings about how second languages are learned in adulthood. This module explores a variety of topics, including the mechanisms in the mind responsible for language acquisition, the roles that input and output play in acquisition, and how language develops in the learner's mind over time. Furthermore, the module explores the many factors believed to impact the outcome of SLA, such as the role of the native language, individual differences in aptitude and motivation, and age of acquisition.

Gregory D. Keating is Associate Professor of Linguistics in the Department of Linguistics and Asian/Middle Eastern Languages at San Diego State University, USA.

The Routledge E-Modules on Contemporary Language Teaching

Series Editors: Bill VanPatten, *Michigan State University, USA*, and Gregory D. Keating, *San Diego State University, USA*

http://routledgetextbooks.com/textbooks/9781315679594/

The *Routledge E-Modules on Contemporary Language Teaching* series is an exciting and innovative approach to topics for the novice or in-training teacher of languages. Written in an easily accessible style and delivered in e-format and paperback versions, specialists and experts provide the latest thinking on a variety of issues that form the foundation of language-teacher knowledge and practice: the nature of language and communication, second language acquisition, interactive tasks, assessment, focus on form, vocabulary development, technology in language teaching, among many others. Each module serves as a self-contained unit to be used on its own or as part of an introductory course on language teaching. Instructors may "mix and match" modules to create their own readings for a course on language teaching. The modules may serve as primary reading or as supplemental reading, with each module offering points of reflection, discussion questions, self-quizzes, and a reading list for those who wish to delve further into the topic.

Language
By Bill VanPatten

Communication and Skill
By Bill VanPatten

Second Language Acquisition: The Basics
By Gregory D. Keating

Vocabulary in Language Teaching
By Joe Barcroft

Interactive Tasks
By Michael J. Leeser and Justin P. White

Focusing on Form in Language Instruction
By Wynne Wong and Daphnée Simard

Technology in Language Learning: An Overview
By Bryan Smith

Teaching Second Language Writing
By Charlene Polio

Content-Based Language Teaching
By Roy Lyster

Second Language Acquisition
The Basics

Gregory D. Keating

Routledge
Taylor & Francis Group

NEW YORK AND LONDON

First published in paperback 2018

First published 2016
by Routledge
711 Third Avenue, New York, NY 10017

and by Routledge
2 Park Square, Milton Park, Abingdon, Oxon, OX14 4RN

Routledge is an imprint of the Taylor & Francis Group, an informa business

Library of Congress Cataloging-in-Publication Data
Names: Keating, Gregory D.
Title: Second language acquisition : the basics / Gregory D. Keating, San Diego State University.
Description: New York, NY : Routledge, 2017. | Series: The Routledge e-modules on contemporary language teaching | Includes bibliographical references.
Identifiers: LCCN 2017024482 | ISBN 9781138500891 (pbk.) | ISBN 9781317394594 (web pdf) | ISBN 9781317394587 (epub) | ISBN 9781317394570 (mobipocket/kindle)
Subjects: LCSH: Second language acquisition.
Classification: LCC P118.2 .K43 2017 | DDC 418.0071—dc23
LC record available at https://lccn.loc.gov/2017024482

ISBN: 978-1-138-50089-1 (pbk)
ISBN: 978-1-315-67957-0 (ebk)

Typeset in Sabon
by Apex CoVantage, LLC

Visit the companion website: http://routledgetextbooks.com/textbooks/9781315679594/

Second Language Acquisition
The Basics

Gregory D. Keating

SAN DIEGO STATE UNIVERSITY

Overview

In this module you will explore the following topics:

- the internal mechanisms responsible for language acquisition
- input and its relationship to internal mechanisms
- language development over time
- factors that affect the outcomes of SLA
- how the above information can be used to inform contemporary language teaching

---

As I began to write this module, I recalled an early experience in my second language teaching career that I wish I could erase from memory. I was a beginning Spanish instructor with little teacher training and no background in second language acquisition (SLA). Like many novice teachers, I wanted to build rapport with my students by making class fun. One day, I decided to play a game that I learned from another student teacher called verb relays. To play the game, the instructor calls out a verb in its unconjugated form (e.g., the Spanish verb *hablar* 'to speak'). The students, who are seated in rows facing the blackboard, must conjugate the verb in all of its person-number forms as quickly as possible in relay form. The first student in each row runs to the blackboard, picks up the chalk, and writes the first-person singular verb form (*hablo* 'I speak'). That person returns to their seat and passes the chalk to the second person in the row, who then runs to the blackboard and writes the second-person singular form (*hablas* 'you speak'), and so on. The row that legibly writes all six person-number forms the fastest wins the relay. We played several rounds. The students liked it. Some even broke a sweat! It was a good teaching day, or so I thought at the time.

In reality, verb relays did more for my students' cardiovascular health than they did for their acquisition of Spanish verbs. My instructional efforts at the time were not informed by research on how languages are learned and, consequently, most of those efforts were not conducive to acquisition. With even a basic knowledge of SLA, I would have been better equipped to evaluate *what* I was doing in the classroom and *why* I was doing it. This module explores some of the basic facts that every language teacher ought to know about how second languages (L2s) are *learned*. Emphasis is placed on the term *learned* because research in the field of SLA focuses on acquisition, not teaching. However, the findings of SLA research have implications for instruction. The focus of this module rests on adult-aged learners, where "adult" refers to an individual who begins L2 acquisition after the first language (L1) is acquired and stabilized; that is, after age 10 or so. Specifically, we'll address the following questions: What components and processes are involved in adult SLA? How does an L2 develop in the learner's mind/brain over time? What factors affect L2 learning in adulthood? Finally, we'll examine how research in SLA can inform contemporary language teaching. Let's begin with the key "ingredients" involved in acquisition.

SLA: The Ingredients

As can be gleaned from any readings on linguistics and the nature of language, language is defined as an implicit and abstract mental representation that humans use to interpret and express meaning. The mental representations that end up in people's minds are of a different nature than the rules of thumb commonly found in textbooks and prescriptive grammars. Language scientists who study acquisition are interested in how humans acquire implicit and abstract mental representations. SLA is a field of inquiry that studies how humans acquire a mental representation of another language after the first has already been acquired. Before we proceed, it is helpful to clarify some potential confusion about what counts as a "second" language. The term *second language* is often used to refer to any language that is learned after the L1, even if it's not second chronologically. For example, an English speaker in the United States might take two years of French in high school followed by two years of Spanish in college. Chronologically, French is a second language and Spanish is a third language, but both can be considered "second" languages because they were both learned after L1 acquisition was completed.

In addition, some people distinguish between foreign language learning and second language learning. **Foreign language learning** entails learning a non-native language in an environment in which it is not the majority language spoken in the community, such as learning Arabic in Japan. In the case of **second language learning**, the non-native language being learned is the majority language spoken in the community, as is the case when learning Arabic in Morocco. This distinction is one of context and the basic findings of SLA research do not differ according to the context of learning. That is, the basic findings of L2 research apply equally to foreign language and L2 contexts. Consequently, in SLA research and in this module, the term *second language* refers to the learning of a non-native language in any context.

Having reviewed what is meant by language, and second language in particular, we are ready to explore how humans acquire the implicit and abstract mental representations that underlie language use. Let's begin by noting that mental representation includes constraints that allow you to know what is possible and impossible in a language. If English is your native language, then you know that the sentence "Who do you wanna call?" is possible, but that the sentence "Who do you wanna call Bill?" is not. Both sentences are fine, though, with *want to* instead of *wanna*. Without training in linguistics, you probably can't explain why contraction of *want to* to *wanna* works in the first sentence but not the second (i.e., your knowledge is abstract), yet you possess an intuition about when the contraction works and when it doesn't (i.e., your knowledge is implicit). How did you come to know this? In infancy and early childhood, you were exposed to spoken English provided by parents and caregivers. Researchers refer to the language that a learner is exposed to as **input**. Internal mechanisms in your mind/brain used English input to build a mental grammar of English. In the field of SLA, all scholars agree that input is a necessary ingredient for acquisition, but there is considerable debate over the nature and design of the internal mechanisms that create the mental grammar. We'll begin with a brief introduction of two competing accounts of the internal mechanisms believed to be responsible for language learning. Then, we'll address the important role that input plays in acquisition.

Internal Mechanisms

Every human possesses what are called domain-general learning mechanisms. These mechanisms allow us to learn a variety of complex mental tasks such as reading, solving arithmetic problems, playing chess, and so forth. Some researchers claim that language is like any other complex mental phenomenon and that it is learned via the same domain-general learning mechanisms that enable us to learn how to program a computer or solve a difficult Sudoku puzzle. This position is widely held by language scientists in psychology and education. Other researchers contend that language is special and is not learned in the same way as other complex mental phenomena. Their claim is that humans are genetically hardwired to learn language and possess additional cognitive mechanisms specifically designed to deal with language, ones separate from the domain-general variety. This viewpoint receives most of its support from linguists. We can refer to the two types of internal mechanisms as **domain-general** and **language-specific**. Because both types are claimed to explain language learning, regardless of whether it's an L1 or L2, we'll refer more generally to *language learning* or *language acquisition* throughout this section. However, along the way, we'll point out the important ways in which L2 learning differs from L1 learning. Let's examine how language learning happens under the domain-general proposal first.

Proponents of domain-general language learning claim that humans are rational problem solvers who construct language by analyzing the input they are exposed to and extracting relevant patterns from it, just like someone who's never played tennis before can figure out how the game is played and scored by watching lots of tennis matches. Under this account, the human mind is a massive data cruncher whose job is to detect linguistic forms in the input—lexical items, inflections, syntactic configurations, and so forth—and tally their frequency of occurrence. After implicitly tallying enough data, the mechanisms will detect patterns where they exist and form implicit generalizations or rules to account for them. Because the mechanisms are not provided in advance with information about how language works, the rules are said to "emerge" in the mind/brain of the learner. We can illustrate this with the example of *want-to* contraction mentioned previously, but we should first review the facts about when *want-to* contraction is possible. Consider the sentences in (1).

(1a) I want to call Bill.
(1b) Who do you want to call?
(1c) Who do you wanna call?

Now consider the sentences in (2).

(2a) I want Michael to call Bill.
(2b) Who do you want to call Bill?
(2c) *Who do you wanna call Bill?

Contraction sounds fine in (1c) but not in (2c). A simple, albeit superficial, way of describing the difference in grammaticality between (1c) and (2c) is to describe it in terms of which syntactic category (subject or object) can move to the front of the sentence if the word is a *wh–* word (e.g., *who, what, when*); that is, we can consider that (1b) is actually *You want to call who?* and that the *who* moves to the front of the sentence to yield *Who do you want to call?* (along with some other minor variations). In (1c), *who* is the direct object of *call*—it refers to Bill. In (2c), *who* is the subject of *call*—it refers to Michael. *Want to* can only contract to form *wanna* when the direct object is fronted, but not when the subject is. Proponents of domain-general language learning would argue that humans can figure this out from their exposure to English input in which *want to* and *wanna* appear. When the *want to* pattern depicted in (1a) and (1b) is noticed in the input, internal learning mechanisms will begin to tally it. The same goes for the *want NP to* pattern depicted in (2a) and for occurrences of *wanna,* such as those shown in (1c). Over time, the learning mechanisms will discover that *wanna* is only possible—or much more likely to occur—with the *want to* pattern. A generalization or rule will emerge: contraction is possible with *want to*, but not with *want NP to*.

To be clear, the learning process described here is largely implicit. A learner might consciously notice a form in the input, but all subsequent tallying and rule emergence happen outside of conscious awareness. You are not consciously aware of how many times you've read the word *the* in this module, or even in this sentence, but the idea is that your internal mechanisms tallied every instance of it. A potential problem for L2 learning is that during the course of L1 acquisition, one's tallying mechanisms become 'tuned' to handle L1 input, which may differ considerably from L2 input. Korean, for example, does not have morphological equivalents for the English plural –*s* or the third-person singular –*s*. Korean-speaking ESL learners may find it difficult to detect such forms in English input because these meanings in Korean are not conveyed via inflections. If forms can't be detected, they can't be tallied, leaving no data upon which rules could emerge. We'll return to this issue in the section on input in this module.

In contrast, proponents of language-specific learning mechanisms claim that input often provides limited, ambiguous, or conflicting evidence about what is possible in a language. For example, English speakers don't hear ungrammatical sentences such as (2c) above and they aren't taught that these sentences are ungrammatical. Nevertheless, English speakers possess intuitions about when contraction is and isn't possible. The idea that humans acquire knowledge of language that could not have resulted from the input to which they were exposed is known as the **poverty-of-the-stimulus** argument. Furthermore, if learners had to figure out language on the basis of input alone, they would produce certain types of non-native structures that are never attested. Based on these claims, proponents of language-specific learning mechanisms argue that domain-general learning mechanisms aren't sufficient for language learning. The language-specific proposal states that humans possess cognitive resources specifically dedicated to language learning and that these resources reside in a different module of the mind than the domain-general variety. Specifically, the claim is that all humans are born with what is called **Universal Grammar**, or **UG** for short. Recent iterations of the theory propose that UG includes an inventory of lexical categories (e.g., noun, verb, adjective) and functional categories (e.g., complementizer, tense) that participate in grammatical operations. Lexical and functional categories form hierarchical phrases in sentences, as shown in (3) below (with technical details omitted):

(3) [$_{CP}$ [$_{TP}$ [$_{VP}$ You saw who]]]

CP stands for complementizer phrase and TP stands for tense phrase, both of which are functional phrases. VP stands for verb phrase, and it is a lexical phrase. Functional phrases are associated with one or more functional features (e.g., number, gender, tense, case), which are also provided as part of the inventory of UG. An example of a functional feature is [wh]. This feature is responsible for *wh-* movement, the grammatical operation that forces question words such as *who* in (1) and (2) above to move from a lower place in a sentence to a higher place. Like all functional features, [wh] is parameterized; that is, some languages make use of it and others do not. The [wh] feature is associated with CPs. It is present in the CPs of languages that have *wh-* movement (e.g., English, Spanish, German) and absent from the CPs of those that don't (e.g., Korean, Chinese). The [wh] features of English CPs, for example, trigger movement of *wh-* words from their base position in the VP up to a position in the CP, as shown in (4) (also with technical details omitted for clarity):

(4) [$_{CP}$ Who [$_{C}$ did [$_{TP}$ [$_{VP}$ you see (e)]]]]

The (e) in (4) stands for an empty category that marks the spot where *who* originated before it moved to the front of the sentence. What does all of this have to do with language learning? Parameterization eases the task of language acquisition by setting limits or constraints on what a possible language can be. That is, due to UG, humans are born 'knowing' (unconsciously, of course) that languages either have *wh-* movement or don't. If the input the learner is exposed to provides evidence that *wh-* movement is present, as fronting of *wh-* words does in English, Spanish, and German, then the [wh] feature in the CP sets to [+wh], where + indicates presence of movement, and the learner's grammar now allows *wh-* fronting. If evidence of *wh-* movement is absent from the input, as is the case in Korean and Chinese, the feature is set to [-wh], where - means absence of movement. In this case, the learner's grammar will not allow *wh-* movement. Language learning, then, amounts to setting functional features to values that are appropriate for the language being learned, with the appropriate value chosen based on the availability of a relevant cue or trigger in the input.

UG provides the learner with other constraints, such as locality constraints on movement. A detailed account is beyond the scope of this discussion, but locality constraints basically inform learners about certain types of movements that are not possible, *so that they don't have to learn them from the input.* That is, UG provides learners with a constraint that allows them to unconsciously know when *wh-* movement is possible, as in (5b) and (5c) below, and, more importantly, when it is not, as in (6d).

(5a) Michael called Bill.
(5b) Who did Michael call?
(5c) Who called Bill?

(6a) Michael called Bill and Greg.
(6b) Who did Michael call?
(6c) Who called Bill and Greg?
(6d) *Who did Michael call and Greg?

The benefit of constraints is that they reduce the number of incorrect hypotheses that learners would surely make about language if they were trying to figure it out on the basis of input alone. If learners were trying to figure out when they could front a *wh-* word and when they couldn't, they'd eventually make the error in (6d), yet child and adult learners of English never do. UG was initially proposed to explain how children learn their L1 so quickly and on the basis of very limited input. Returning to the *wanna* example, English-speaking children acquire the constraints on want-to contraction as early as age two. It's doubtful that two-year-olds have heard enough sentences with *want to* and *wanna* to have figured out when want-to contraction is not possible. But they could learn something this abstract and complex if UG supplied relevant knowledge, which in the case of *wanna* is captured by trace theory. Trace theory is related to the [wh] feature and locality constraints and, in simple terms, says that whenever a *wh-* word moves to a higher position in the sentence, it leaves behind a silent and invisible copy of itself called a *trace* (silent because traces aren't audible in spoken input and invisible because traces aren't printed in standard written input). To illustrate, see sentences (7) and (8) below, which are repetitions of (1b) and (2b) above, this time with the movement traces shown as italicized *t*s.

(7) Who$_i$ do you want to call t_i?
(8) Who$_i$ do you want t_i to call Bill?

The trace essentially indicates that even though *who* has moved to the front of the sentence, an empty trace of it still remains in its original location. Traces explain why want-to contraction is possible in (7), but not in (8). In (7), nothing intervenes between *want* and *to,* leaving them free to contract. In (8), a movement trace (i.e., a silent copy of *who*) intervenes between the two, effectively blocking contraction. Humans 'know' this because knowledge of traces is part of UG. Once the *wh-* feature of the CP is set to [+wh], knowledge of trace theory is activated and no additional exposure to input is needed to know that want-to contraction is not permissible in sentences like (8). This explains why children can learn the constraints on something abstract and complex like want-to contraction before they have control over grammatical morphemes, which abound in the input. It also explains why humans learn a variety of other phenomena at roughly the same time, such as contractions with modals and auxiliaries, as in the examples below:

(9) I've done it.
(10) *Should I've done it?

Sentence (9) probably sounds fine to you, whereas the alternate version in (10) probably strikes you as a 'bad' English sentence. Why is contraction possible in the first sentence but not the second? To form the second sentence, the modal *should* raises from a base position between *I* and *have*, leaving behind a trace, as in (11):

(11) Shouldi I t_i have done it?

Contraction in (11) is forbidden for the same reason that it is in (8). Language-specific mechanisms provide the learner with knowledge about traces, which allows them to learn multiple structures 'for free,' including contractions with *want to*, modals, auxiliaries, copular verbs, and pronouns. Under a domain-general learning account, each type of contraction has to be learned separately.

Language learning via innate mechanisms, such as UG, is also implicit. In this case, learners are not consciously aware that they possess functional categories or locality constraints, nor are they aware of the particular values of features that form part of their grammar. L2 learning involves re-setting parameterized features from L1 values to L2 values (where the L1 and L2 differ) as well as figuring out which features and constraints from UG apply to the L2. For example, a Korean-speaking learner of ESL needs to reset the *wh-* feature from [-wh] to [+wh] and activate their inborn knowledge of movement traces, neither of which were relevant to learning Korean because Korean lacks *wh-* movement. There are at least two potential problems for learning parameterized features in SLA. The first is that innate knowledge that doesn't apply to the L1 may not be available for L2 learning later in life. Even if it is, a second potential problem is that L2 learners may not be able to detect the relevant cue or trigger in the input that would bring about the required change in feature values. These issues will be addressed in later sections of this module.

Reflection

When two theories 'compete' to explain something, one often feels compelled to choose a side. That is, one must either believe that humans possess innate knowledge of language or believe that they don't (take as evidence the strong division between psychologists and linguists on issues related to the nature of language). It's also possible that some aspects of language are learned via innate mechanisms and others are learned via domain-general mechanisms. Do any of the following components of language seem more likely to be learned via one type of mechanism than the other: (a) phonemic contrasts such as /r/ vs. /l/; (b) nominal and verbal inflections; (c) content and function words; (d) syntax; (e) pragmatic aspects of language, such as politeness?

To summarize, under the domain-general account, language learning amounts to a statistical learning problem that involves extracting patterns from input. Under the language-specific account, acquisition involves setting the values of inborn parameters based on triggers in the input, and activating related principles. As you read more about acquisition, you'll form your own opinion about which account better explains language learning. There is quite a bit of evidence for and against each account and both have challenges to overcome. For the domain-general proposal to win out, it needs to be shown that the input provides all of the evidence learners need to construct the highly abstract and complex stuff that winds up in a speaker's mental representation for language, including what is not possible in a given language. Explanations are also needed for why highly frequent forms aren't always learned before less frequent ones. For the language-specific proposal to prevail, it needs to explain why parameter re-setting in adult SLA isn't as uniform as it is in L1 acquisition. ESL learners, for example, have been shown to be inconsistent and variable when tested on the constraints on want-to contraction, despite being very native-like when tested on knowledge of the constraints on *wh-* movement. This and similar evidence has led some researchers to propose that L1 acquisition is guided by language-specific mechanisms, whereas L2 learning is guided by domain-general mechanisms, which are more subject to individual differences.

Regardless of which account ultimately wins out, it is clear that input is a necessary ingredient for the creation of mental representations. Input is the driving force behind the tallying and rule emergence that lie at the heart of domain-general explanations for language learning, and is the catalyst for the learning of parameterized features advocated by proponents of language-specific learning mechanisms. However, to say that internal mechanisms need input is as vague as saying that children need food to grow and develop. What kind of input do these mechanisms need? How much input do they need? In the following section, we turn our attention to these and similar questions.

Input

In SLA research, **input** refers to language that a learner hears or reads (or sees in the case of signed language) that has communicative intent.

Communicative intent means that the input contains a message that the learner is supposed to attend to for its meaning. Much of the language that teachers use in their interpersonal communication with students and to manage their classrooms qualifies as input by this definition. When an ESL instructor says, "Please put the exams on my desk" or asks, "Did you turn in a composition?" students get language that they must attend to for meaning and respond to in appropriate ways. Such meaning-bearing input is a crucial source of **primary linguistic data** about how English works. For example, the –s inflection on *exams* expresses the meaning "more than one" and provides evidence of how English encodes this meaning grammatically. The function words *the* and *a* indicate that English has definite and indefinite articles (Russian and Japanese do not), and so on. Input, as defined here, provides the internal mechanisms with data or evidence about how the language works and learning mechanisms use this data to create an implicit linguistic system.

Communicative input of the type described above is often lacking in L2 classrooms. In its place, students receive copious amounts of information *about* the L2. This includes rules of thumb, such as "To form the plural in English, add –s to the noun," models of correct language use, such as "I have one dog, but she has two dogs," and error correction, as in "We say feet, not foots." These uses of language look like input on the surface because they convey meaning (if provided in the L2). However, rules of thumb lack primary linguistic data (i.e., there are no plural nouns that learners must attend to for meaning). Models and error correction contain exemplars of the target form, but learners' attention is diverted entirely toward the forms themselves and away from meaning, which is not the case in the examples of primary linguistic data mentioned above. Also excluded from input are exercises that can be completed without attention to meaning, as when learners hear a list of nouns (e.g., *house, dogs*) and have to state whether they are singular or plural. Learners can complete such activities correctly even when provided with nonsense words such as *wug* and *blicks*. The definition of input provided above also excludes all exercises whose aim is to get learners to produce language (even those that require attention to meaning). This is because the acquisition of an implicit linguistic system is built up by actively trying to *comprehend* meaningful language, not produce it. The expression of meaning-bearing language is called **output.** Output, and the potential role it plays in language acquisition, will be discussed in a later section of this module.

In sum, internal mechanisms can't use information *about* the language, practice aimed at language production, or language that doesn't have to be attended to for its meaning. They can only utilize linguistic data embedded in meaning-bearing language. However, not all of the linguistic data provided in input is immediately available to internal mechanisms. During the act of comprehension, learners, especially at the initial stages of learning, are known to 'filter out' or ignore some of the input they are exposed to. In the following section, we examine how L2 learners process (i.e., how they get linguistic data from) the input they are exposed to.

Input Processing

L2 learners often come to the task of acquisition with comprehension strategies that cause them to filter out or ignore linguistic data in the input, the very data that the internal mechanisms need to create an implicit system. Consider the exchange below between a beginning ESL learner, Jung Soo, and his college roommate, David, who is a native English speaker:

JUNG SOO: What you do last night?
DAVID: I downloaded songs from iTunes.

David's response to Jung Soo's question constitutes input. It's language that Jung Soo hears and that he must attend to for its meaning. In his reply, David uses the linguistic means of expression afforded to him by English: lexical items, verbal and nominal inflections, prepositions, and so forth. Jung Soo's job is to comprehend the meaning of what David says, which involves decoding how David conveyed meaning. That is, Jung Soo must attend to the linguistic forms in David's response and attach meaning to them, a process known as making **form-meaning connections**. This is not an easy thing to do, given that this is a conversation and David speaks at a normal rate, like he would with his English-speaking friends. In an attempt to comprehend what he can, Jung Soo will do what all beginning learners do: he'll focus on what he perceives to be content words in the input and will attempt to attach meaning to them to get the gist of what David says. Given that content words convey most of what a sentence means, this is a highly reliable comprehension strategy for beginning L2 learners. However, by attempting to identify and get meaning from content words alone, Jung Soo ignores crucial pieces of inflectional morphology, such as the past tense inflection on the verb and the plural inflection on the noun, and he probably also ignores function words like the preposition *from*. He does not do this consciously or intentionally. He simply doesn't have the capacity to attend to all of the linguistic data in the input in real time (i.e., in the moment in which the input is perceived). The subset of data that learners are able to attend to and hold in working memory for further processing is called **intake**. For comparative purposes, the sentences below depict the input that Jung Soo was exposed to and the intake that he was likely able to derive from it during real time (i.e., moment-by-moment) sentence comprehension.

INPUT: I downloaded songs from iTunes.
INTAKE: I download song (from) iTunes.

A major difficulty learners face is that lexical items often take on the work of grammatical forms when processing for meaning. For example, imagine that David had replied to Jung Soo in the following way: *Last night I downloaded several songs from iTunes*. Here the meanings of "action in the past" and "more than one" are conveyed not only by inflections, but also by lexical items (the adverb *last night* and the quantifier *several*, respectively). Because lexical items convey most of the semantic information that learners need to understand a sentence, their presence only reinforces learners' natural strategy of relying on content words and ignoring the grammatical forms that carry the same meaning. In research on input processing, this tendency to rely on content words at the expense of grammatical forms when both encode the same meaning is called the **lexical preference strategy**.

Reflection

Do you think form-meaning connections are easier to make in one type of input (e.g., spoken language) vs. another (e.g., written language)? What factors of spoken or written language make it more or less difficult to detect a form and connect it to meaning?

At the same time that comprehension requires listeners/readers to make form-meaning connections, it also requires them to determine the syntactic relationships among words in a sentence, such as whether a noun phrase is the subject or object of a verb. Assigning syntactic structure to a sentence during comprehension is called **parsing**. The English verb *hug*, for example, assigns two semantic roles: agent (the entity that performs an action) and patient (the entity that is acted upon). Because word order in English is SVO, determining agent/patient roles is very straightforward. The noun that precedes the verb is the subject/agent and the noun that comes after is the object/patient, as in (12).

(12) The man hugged the woman.

One exception to this tendency is the passive construction, shown in (13).

(13) The man was hugged by the woman.

In (13), the NP *the man* is still the subject of *hugged*, but it's not the agent; rather, it's the patient. Beginning learners of English misinterpret sentences like (13) to mean *The man hugged the woman*, even when their L1 forms passives in a similar way. This tendency to assume that the first noun is the subject/agent is called the **first-noun strategy**.

The foregoing discussion highlights some important facts. First, if linguistic data in the input is not processed—that is, if a form is not detected and connected to meaning—it doesn't get delivered to the internal mechanisms that need it. Only input that has been processed—that is, only *intake*—is made available to internal mechanisms. Second, intake may contain incorrect evidence about the L2, as happens when ESL learners assume that the first NP in a passive sentence is the agent, or when learners assign an incorrect meaning to a form. More information about input processing can be found in the *Suggestions for further reading* at the end of this module. Lastly, internal mechanisms have to make do with what they get. If the intake only consists of content words, as it does for most beginning L2 learners, then that's the data the internal mechanisms have to work with and they'll build whatever linguistic representations they can until additional data are made available to them. As new data are received, new representations are built and/or ones previously built may be revised. In short, the implicit linguistic system is dynamic; that is, it is constantly changing. At the same time that SLA is dynamic, it is also slow. For some aspects of language, particularly morphological inflections, copious amounts of input may be needed for acquisition, far more than what most learners are likely to receive in L2 classrooms. In the following section, we delve into how language develops in the learner's mind/brain over time.

Quiz

Take the following short quiz to see what you have learned so far. Answers are given at the end, so don't peek.

1. Which of the following scenarios constitutes foreign language learning?

   a. learning Portuguese in Brazil
   b. learning Farsi (Persian) in the United States
   c. both a and b

2. According to domain-general accounts, language learning . . .

   a. depends on frequency in the input.
   b. involves recognizing patterns in the input.
   c. both a and b

3. Proponents of language-specific learning mechanisms believe that . . .

   a. humans are genetically equipped to learn language.
   b. humans know things about language that go beyond the input.
   c. both a and b

4. Which of the following statements about parameterized features is TRUE?

   a. All languages set the value of a feature the same way.
   b. Exposure to input is needed to set parameters appropriately.
   c. They are part of our domain-general learning mechanisms.

5. Which of the following constitutes input for acquisition of the third-person final –*s* in English?

   a. "My dog sleeps all day. I think most dogs sleep all day."
   b. "Remember that English puts –*s* on third-person verbs."
   c. "Class, repeat after me: I walk, he walks."

6. Which statement about intake is TRUE?

   a. Intake is what internal mechanisms use to build an implicit system.
   b. Intake for beginning learners is a subset of the input.
   c. both a and b

7. Which of the following sentences contains an inflection that is redundant (i.e., an inflection that expresses a meaning that is conveyed elsewhere in the sentence)?

   a. Mark ate our cookies.
   b. Mark's sweater is black.
   c. Mark runs in the park.

8. Learners of Spanish tend to misinterpret OVS sentences. Which principle of input processing explains why?

   a. the first-noun strategy
   b. the lexical preference principle
   c. neither a nor b

[Answers: 1. b; 2. c; 3. c; 4. b; 5. a; 6. c; 7. c; 8. a]

Language Development

Having established that language acquisition is input-driven and that intake, and not the raw input per se, is what is made available to internal learning mechanisms, some interesting questions arise: What happens after a form-meaning connection is made? What sorts of changes take place in the learner's linguistic system as new form-meaning connections (i.e., new intake data) are made available to learning mechanisms? How do learners tap their developing system for language use? These and similar questions speak to *language development*. In this section, we focus on development from two perspectives: (1) the growth or creation of the implicit linguistic system in the learner's mind over time; and (2) development of the abilities to access that system for speech production. Let's start with the development of the learner's mental grammar.

Development of the Implicit Linguistic System

Development of the implicit system involves at least two processes: accommodation and restructuring. In our discussion of input processing, we defined intake as linguistic data in the input that learners attend to and hold in working memory for further processing. As the phrase *for further processing* suggests, making form-meaning connections is just the initial stage in the acquisition of grammatical form. When a learner links a form in the input, such as the English word *dog* (pronounced [dɔg]) to its meaning (i.e., four-legged canine that barks), the resulting form-meaning connection is a candidate for accommodation. **Accommodation** refers to the integration of new language data into the learner's developing system. Accommodation can happen all at once, or in stages. Suppose, for example, that an ESL learner first hears the word *dog* as part of the two-word phrase *dog grooming*. Given that the last sound in *dog* and the first sound in *grooming* are the same, the learner could mistakenly segment the input as being *do grooming* (pronounced [dɔ gru:miŋ]) and link the meaning of "four-legged canine that barks" to the sound sequence [dɔ]. In this case, the learner might accommodate the initial consonant and the subsequent vowel in *dog*, but not the final consonant, [g]. Subsequent exposures to the word *dog* in other contexts, such as hearing the word in isolation or followed by a word that begins with a different sound (e.g., *dog food*), would provide the learner with the input needed to add the final sound to the lexical entry. Once the final sound is added, the form would be fully accommodated.

Once accommodated, *dog* will connect with other nouns in the system, as well as with words that can combine with nouns, such as the articles *the* and *a*. Psycholinguists currently conceive of the mental lexicon as a vast network of lexical items and surface inflections that are interconnected. The connections that a word has with other words and inflections vary in strength based on root form, meaning, frequency of co-occurrence in the input, and other factors. For example, although *dog* and *cat* are derived from different roots, the connection between them is likely to be strong given that they share similar meanings (i.e., both are four-legged, domesticated house pets) and often co-occur in the input (i.e., we are more likely to hear the word *cat* in a conversation about *dogs* than in a conversation about *cars*). Similarly, there would be a weaker connection between *dog* and *spoon*, given that these two nouns have different roots and meanings and are less likely to co-occur in the input.

In the initial stages of word learning, lexical items are accommodated on an item-by-item basis. Thus, in a beginning learner's linguistic system, there might be entries for singular nouns such as *dog*, *cat*, and *house*, and separate entries for the corresponding plural forms *dogs*, *cats*, and *houses*. Over time, as new intake is accommodated, data across the entire system will get reorganized in new ways. This process is known as **restructuring**. Continuing the example of the English plural, when an ESL learner begins to link the –*s* inflection on nouns to its meaning during comprehension, the resulting intake will lead to accommodation of the plural –*s* as a unique form in the mental lexicon with its own meaning. Once accommodated, the plural –*s* will form new connections with singular nouns in the system, such as *dog*, *cat*, and *house*. This obviates the need to have separate lexical entries for plural nouns that take –*s*, such as *dogs* and *houses*, so these will eventually be deleted. Initially, the plural morpheme may form connections with every noun in the system, including singular nouns that don't form the plural with –*s*, such as *foot* and *tooth*, and may also connect with nouns in the system that are already plural, such as the irregular forms *feet* and *teeth*. As the learner continues to receive English input, the connections between –*s* and nouns will either be strengthened or weakened depending on what is attested in the input. Connections made between –*s* and *dog* will be strengthened, whereas those made between –*s* and *foot* or *feet* will be weakened and ultimately deleted because they are not attested in the input. As this example illustrates, the implicit linguistic system is in a state of flux and undergoes both quantitative and qualitative changes during the acquisition process. An important point to make is that input—or rather, intake—is the catalyst that drives change in the system. Without exposure to comprehensible, meaning-bearing input, development of the implicit system will not take place.

Although input is the catalyst for language development, much of the evidence that we have about the changes that occur in the implicit linguistic system has been documented by examining the language that learners produce and how that language changes over time. Many of the initial studies of language development were longitudinal, meaning that learners' speech was recorded and analyzed over long periods of time, usually several months to a couple of years. One interesting finding of this research is that learners often pass through stages on their way to acquiring a particular form or structure. The acquisition of the English plural mentioned above is an example of what are called **developmental stages** or **developmental sequences**. On their way toward native-like use of the plural, ESL learners pass through the following stages:

- Initially, learners do not mark plurality at all, as when a learner says *I bought book*. In the absence of context, it's not clear whether the learner refers to one book (i.e., *I bought [a] book*) or more than one (i.e., *I bought book[s]*).

- Shortly afterwards, learners begin to mark the plural lexically (i.e., with numerals and quantifiers) but not morphologically. Lexically marked plurals include *two dog and *many cat.
- Later on, learners acquire a few regular and irregular plural nouns and use them correctly. They'll say things like *cats* and *feet*, and may appear to have mastery of the plural.
- After a period of using regular and irregular plurals correctly, learners' use of the regular plural increases substantially and results in non-native structures with the irregulars that were not attested earlier, such as saying *foots and *feets.
- Later on, the internal system begins to eradicate the "regularized" irregulars such as *foots and *feets and replace them with the correct irregular forms that they began with.

In this context, the term 'stage' refers to a change in linguistic behavior. That is, learners perform in a particular way for a period of time and then perform in a different way at a later point in time. These changes are gradual and learners often show vestiges of previous stages as they transition to the next. That is, when learners begin to mark the plural morphologically with –s, they'll also continue to frequently omit this inflection. In the acquisition of English as a second language, developmental stages have also been observed with the past tense, negation, and question formation, among other structures. They have also been attested in the acquisition of other L2s such as German, Swedish, and Spanish, among others.

Reflection

A possible interpretation of the stage in which ESL learners begin to produce non-native forms such as *foots and *feets is that they have regressed (i.e., taken a step backward in their learning). Do you agree with this interpretation? Why or why not?

Developmental stages give us a window into how a particular form or structure is acquired, but they tell us nothing about when one form is acquired relative to another. **Acquisition orders** refer to the sequential acquisition of different grammatical forms over time. One of the most well documented acquisition orders in SLA research is the acquisition of English inflectional morphemes and function words. Multiple longitudinal (long term) and cross-sectional (learners at different levels) studies coincide in showing that learners acquire different morphemes and function words at different points in time. Looking across different categories of morphemes and function words, the research shows the following order of acquisition:

- Group 1: present progressive *ing*, plural *–s*, copula
- Group 2: auxiliaries, articles
- Group 3: irregular past
- Group 4: regular past *–ed*, third-person singular *–s*, possessive *–'s*

In these studies, a form was usually said to be 'acquired' if it was supplied in 90% of obligatory contexts across multiple data sampling sessions, often three sessions that were several weeks or months apart. An obligatory context for the plural *–s*, for example, would be the use of a noun followed by a numeral greater than one (e.g., *three* + noun) or a quantifier (e.g., *several* + noun). The groups of morphemes above indicate that learners first meet the 90% accuracy criterion with the present progressive, the plural, and the copula, which are acquired at roughly the same time. This does not mean that learners do not use forms that comprise groups 2, 3, and 4. Learners will use the forms in groups 2, 3, and 4 long before they achieve 90% accuracy with the forms in group 1; they just won't be very accurate with forms that fall outside of group 1 and won't hit the 90% criterion with those forms until after they've reached the criterion with forms lower in the order.

Research on developmental stages and acquisition orders has yielded interesting insights into how second languages are learned. For example, stages of development and acquisition orders do not vary based on learners' native language, the age that L2 learning begins, or the context of acquisition (i.e., classroom vs. non-classroom learning). Perhaps the two most important insights that language teachers can gain from developmental stages and acquisition orders are the following: (1) that acquisition is slow; and (2) that learners need copious amounts of input to pass through developmental sequences and acquisition orders. In order to acquire the English plural, for example, learners likely need several months to a couple of years of continuous exposure to English input to reach the final stage of eliminating regularized irregulars such as **foots* and **feets*. Completing the acquisition order for English morphemes and functions words described above requires several years, regardless of whether learning occurs naturalistically or in classrooms where grammar instruction is provided. This knowledge can help instructors temper their expectations about the speed of learning. Instructors sometimes say things such as "I covered the plural already and my students still make errors," or "I tried using input to teach the plural and it didn't work." Learners will not traverse developmental stages after a day or two of instruction on a particular form. Likewise, input is not a new 'teaching technique' that results in instantaneous acquisition. Developmental stages and acquisition orders tell us that much of language learning is beyond a teacher's (and a learner's) direct control. Learners have to be developmentally ready to learn, much like an infant has to be developmentally ready to progress from crawling to standing and later on from standing to walking and even later on from walking to running.

Development of Speech Production

Although development of the implicit system takes years, L2 learners do not wait until they have acquired a native-like mental representation of the L2 to attempt to communicate. Learners produce meaning-bearing language, also called **output**, from the earliest moments of language learning. Making output involves two processes: (1) accessing the mental lexicon to retrieve the lexical items and grammatical forms needed to express a particular meaning; and (2) putting those items together into coherent sentences via production strategies. Just like the implicit system that learners rely on to make output is under development, learners must also develop production strategies in the L2. One well-articulated theory of L2 speech processing proposes that speech production in an L2 is dependent on acquiring a series of five output procedures. The procedures exist in an implicational hierarchy, which means that the acquisition of each procedure is dependent on having acquired the one that precedes it. A major consequence of this implicational hierarchy is that learners cannot skip stages and the acquisition of procedures; they can only do what they are ready to do. In terms of output, each procedure allows learners to increase the grammatical complexity of their speech. Learners' initial attempts at making output involve retrieving lexical items from the mental lexicon and cobbling them together to make an utterance, a process called *lexical access*. The following sentence is representative of what an ESL learner might say at this early point in development:

(14) David download many song.

It's not entirely surprising that a learner's early output would consist primarily of content words. Content words constitute the bulk of the initial intake that learners derive from input and, consequently, they are the first elements accommodated into the system and made available for output. In order to use morphological inflections and move words around in a sentence, learners must develop specific procedures. The first procedure that learners acquire is the *category procedure*. This procedure enables a learner to add inflections to words, such as adding –*ed* to a verb or the possessive's to a noun (e.g., David's iPhone), but only in cases where the inflection does not agree with something else in the sentence. Having acquired the category procedure, an ESL learner might say the sentence below:

(15) David download*ed* many song.

In this example, the past tense marker *–ed* does not duplicate a meaning conveyed elsewhere in the sentence. In contrast, adding an *–s* to *song* requires agreement between the quantifier *many* and the noun. This requires the more advanced procedure described next.

The next procedure in the hierarchy is the *noun phrase (NP) procedure*, which enables the learner to use inflections in NPs that require agreement, such as number agreement between a quantifier and a noun, as in the example below.

(16) David downloaded many song*s*.

So, whereas the category procedure enables a learner to add *–s* to *songs* in a sentence in which the plural *–s* does not agree with anything else, such as *David downloaded songs*, the learner must acquire the NP procedure to use the same morpheme in NPs that require agreement. In Romance languages, the NP procedure is what allows learners to make gender and number agreement between nouns and adjectives in phrases such as *casa*$_N$ *roja*$_{ADJ}$ 'red house' and *casas*$_N$ *rojas*$_{ADJ}$ 'red houses.'

Following the noun phrase procedure is the *verb phrase (VP) procedure*. This procedure enables the learner to move elements from within the VP to the beginning of the sentence. This procedure allows an ESL learner, for example, to front adverbs, as in *Yesterday David downloaded many songs*, and to form inverted *wh-* questions, such as the one below:

(17) **What songs** David download?

The next procedure in the hierarchy is the *sentence procedure*, also called the *S-procedure*, which enables the learner to make agreement across two phrases, such as between an NP and a VP. This enables learners of Spanish to make gender and number agreement between nouns and predicative adjectives (i.e., adjectives that appear in the VP), such as *Las casas son rojas* 'The houses are red.' The sentence procedure is also what allows ESL learners to make subject-verb agreement, as in the example below:

(18) David download*s* many songs.

In this example, *David* is a third-person singular subject and therefore requires a verb with the same features. Even though the words are adjacent to one another, as are *many* and *songs*, subject-verb agreement is more difficult because it happens across a phrasal boundary (i.e., between an NP and VP) instead of within a phrase.

The final procedure in the hierarchy is the subordinate *clause procedure*, which enables the learner to match features across a clause boundary, such as ensuring that the gender of a pronoun (e.g., *he*) in a subordinate clause matches the gender of its antecedent NP (e.g., *David*) in a main clause, as in the example below.

(19) **David** said that **he** downloaded many songs.

In this example, the main clause is *David said* and the subordinate clause is *that he downloaded many songs*. Agreement in this case happens across clauses. The subordinate clause procedure is also involved in Romance languages in which information in the main clause triggers use of the subjunctive mood in subordinate clauses.

Unlike research on acquisition orders, which places great importance on the accuracy of use of individual morphemes, the theory of L2 speech processing described above focuses on the acquisition of the procedures themselves, not the individual forms that a procedure enables a learner to produce. For example, the category procedure is required to produce several English morphemes, such as the present progressive, the plural, the past, and the possessive. Showing productive use of any one of these inflections would suffice to claim that a learner has acquired the procedure. By *productive use* we mean that a learner has produced the form a certain number of times in a variety of different constructions across two or more data samples. This does not mean that the learner will have a high degree of accuracy with that form, or with any of the others that the learner could conceivably produce with that procedure. Likewise, learners will continue to acquire new procedures in the hierarchy before achieving native-like use of forms that require procedures lower in the hierarchy. So, an ESL learner will likely acquire the NP procedure before achieving a high level of accuracy on any or all of the forms subsumed under the category procedure.

Reflection

What implications do stages of development, acquisition orders, and the development of L2 speech processing procedures have for second language instruction?

The Role of Output in Acquisition

Up to now, we have stressed the critical role that input plays in the acquisition of mental representation. We have seen that it plays a fundamental role in everything from vocabulary development to syntax to morphological development. In fact, there is no facet of language for which input does not play a major contributing role in its acquisition. A question that some people ask is "What about output? Does having to produce language play some kind of role in language acquisition?" Output does play a role, but the stance taken in this module is that it does not play the same role as input. Whereas input drives development of the implicit system, output contributes to the development of skill. In the case of language, **skill** refers to the ability to use language fluently, which means with little error and effort. Put differently, output hones a learner's ability to *access* the implicit system with accuracy and speed, but it does not develop the implicit knowledge in the system. That is, one's own act of accessing the developing system to produce the English plural, for example, does not contribute to the acquisition of a mental representation for the plural –*s*. Rather, one's ability to produce the plural –*s* during interaction indicates that the plural has already been accommodated into the developing system, hence its availability for use during language production. Opportunities to produce the plural in meaning-bearing language develop the learner's skill in accessing that form during spontaneous language use.

In addition to its role in skill development, producing speech in the L2 may draw learners' attention to grammatical forms or structures that they need to acquire. For example, in response to a question about a New Year's Eve celebration, a learner may wish to say *I saw fireworks*, but not know the word for *fireworks* in the L2. The learner might proceed to test a hypothesis about what the correct form is, or ask the interlocutor for the word. Output may also make learners aware of language that they've learned incorrectly, as when a learner says "skater board" and later hears a native speaker say "skateboard." Furthermore, when learners attempt to convey meanings that are not clearly understood by an interlocutor, they often get **feedback** on their output, which refers to information about the incorrectness of their utterances. In normal communication, this feedback is implicit rather than explicit. It may consist of requests for clarification such as *Huh?* or *What?*, confirmations of what an interlocutor believes the L2 learner said (e.g., "Did you say skateboard?"), or attempts to restate a learner's incorrectly formed utterance but with the errors removed, as when a learner says, "I got a new skater board" and an interlocutor replies, "You got a new skateboard." As some of these examples show, feedback may contain additional input on a form that is problematic for the learner, which may push them to become better processors of input.

In sum, like the development of the implicit linguistic system, developing the ability to access the system to make output takes a considerable amount of time. Nevertheless, the developmental phenomena discussed above suggest that there is a high degree of uniformity in how humans learn languages. That is, all learners, regardless of the L1 they speak and the L2 they are learning, must acquire the same five procedures to make output and must acquire them in the same order. Likewise, all learners of English as a second language will acquire the present progressive and the plural before acquiring past tense and third-person singular. At the same time, learners vary in how fast they progress through stages and acquisition orders. There is also a high degree of variability in how far people get in language learning. In the following section, we address some of the factors believed to affect the development and the ultimate outcome of adult SLA.

Factors that Affect Acquisition

One observation often made about adult SLA is that the outcome is not uniform across individuals. Some learners acquire mental representations of the L2 that are native-like, whereas others seem not to. Likewise, some learners achieve high levels of ability in comprehension and/or production, whereas others do not. Variability is also found across linguistic subsystems; that is, at a given point in time, a learner may be further along in the development of one component of language, such as syntax, than in another, such as morphology or phonology. Of the many factors believed to explain at least some of the variable outcomes of SLA, we'll touch on the following: age of onset of L2 learning, transfer from the L1, individual differences in learning ability, and instruction. Let's begin with the age factor.

Age of Onset of L2 Acquisition

Whereas every human's first exposure to an L1 occurs at or around birth (including simultaneous bilingualism), one's initial exposure to an L2 can occur at any point during the lifespan. Is there an advantage to learning an L2 earlier in life rather than later? Most people seem to think so. It's quite common to hear people make statements such as "Children are better language learners than adults" or "If you want to learn a language, you have to start when you're young." The effect that age has on L2 learning has received considerable attention in SLA research. It's important to clarify which components or processes involved in acquisition are thought to be affected by age. If much of language acquisition results from the interaction between input and internal learning mechanisms, which is mediated by input processing, it stands to reason that age either affects the internal mechanisms responsible for language learning, the learners' ability to process input, or both. Most claims about age effects in SLA have centered on the internal learning mechanisms responsible for language learning. Specifically, the issue that has been raised is whether the human capacity to learn language is available throughout the lifespan, or only during a so-called **critical period**. To say that language is bound by a critical period means that there is a biologically determined window of time during which humans can acquire language. If initial exposure to input begins after the end of this time window, language acquisition will not be fully native-like, no matter how much input one receives after initial exposure. The hypothesized critical period for language learning begins at birth and is said to end in late childhood or early adolescence. Given this scenario, a learner is deemed capable of achieving native-like abilities in an L2 if initial exposure begins before late childhood (i.e., before age 10 or so), but not if first exposure occurs after this age. This would seem to preclude most adult-aged L2 learners—as we defined 'adult' at the outset of this module—from achieving native-like abilities. What does SLA research have to say about all of this?

The consensus in the field is that age indeed affects L2 acquisition. However, this does not entail that there is a critical period for SLA and the available evidence strongly suggests that there isn't one. If language learning in adulthood were subject to a critical period that ends in early adolescence, starting acquisition at any age after the cut-off should result in similar outcomes. That is, starting at age 20 should be no better than starting at age 40 because both starting points occur after the end of the purported critical period. This is not what most studies show. When learners' age of initial exposure to the L2 is correlated with their performance on test measures, the results show that outcomes decline steadily as age of onset of acquisition increases. That is, starting at age 10 is better than starting at age 20, which is better than starting at 30, and so on throughout the lifespan. Some recent research suggests that the decline may begin as early as a year or two after birth. This is not the pattern typical of a critical period. Rather, this pattern strongly suggests that some of the variable outcomes of SLA are due to the amount of time one is exposed to the L2 (i.e., the quantity and quality of interaction that a person has in the language). A 30-year-old learner of Spanish who starts at age 10 gets 10 more years of exposure to the L2 than another 30-year-old learner who begins at age 20. This is a significant difference in time on task. So, it's never too late to begin learning a new language, but the later one starts, the less likely one is to receive the copious amounts of input and interaction with speakers required to achieve native-like abilities.

Reflection

Research in SLA has yet to study the effects that age of onset of acquisition has on a learner's ability to process input. Which of the following factors associated with normal aging do you think could affect how older adults process input: (a) decreased working memory capacity; (b) slower processing speed; (c) decreased attention in dual task conditions (e.g., watching TV and talking on the phone); (d) loss of hearing; (e) loss of vision?

In spite of the evidence against a biologically determined cut-off age for language learning, the construct of a critical period still has currency in SLA research. Some theories of adult language learning incorporate critical periods into their explanations of non-native outcomes, but the claims are much more nuanced and are often restricted to particular components of language (e.g., phonology but not syntax) or subsets of language features. For example, one hypothesis claims that adult learners of L2s cannot acquire native-like knowledge or use of grammatical structures not present in the L1. Under this account, Italian-speaking learners of L2 Spanish are predicted to acquire native-like representations of Spanish gender because Italian, like Spanish, has grammatical gender. In contrast, English-speaking learners are deemed incapable of acquiring native-like outcomes with grammatical gender because English lacks an analogous system. These claims have been the subject of much debate in one line of SLA research. A growing body of evidence suggests that gender is acquirable in an L2 regardless of its presence in the L1, contra the critical period claim. In any event, this version of a critical period proposal raises a variable worthy of its own discussion: the role of the L1 in SLA.

The L1

Questions about the role that the L1 plays in SLA are essentially questions about the starting point, or the **initial state**, of L2 learning. The initial state refers to what learners start out with in advance of receiving input. In L1 acquisition, an infant's initial state consists of internal learning mechanisms and any universal processing strategies that humans have for attending to input. After a few years of exposure to input, children build a mental grammar that accounts for the L1 and acquire processing routines appropriate for handling L1 input. What, then, is the starting point for SLA? Do learners transfer the grammatical properties and processing strategies of the L1, or do they default to the initial state resembling that which existed prior to their L1 acquisition? Researchers are not in complete agreement on the answer to this question, and there are also 'hybrid' proposals that advocate partial transfer. Nevertheless, the prevailing view—and the one that has the most empirical support across theoretical frameworks—is that the L1 is the starting point for L2 acquisition. In terms of the grammar, this means that L2 learners transfer grammatical properties of the L1 into the L2 and must learn the appropriate L2 properties. We can illustrate this with a grammatical property called headedness. Some languages, like English, are head-first, meaning that heads of phrases appear before other information in the phrase. Other languages, such as Japanese, are head-final, meaning that heads of phrases appear at the ends of phrases. This results in a number of word order differences between the two languages. For example, word order in English VPs is VO, as in *Taro is eating an apple*. In Japanese, word order is OV, as in *Taro apple is eating*. Similarly, in English, prepositions precede nouns, as in *in the kitchen*. In Japanese, the equivalent words come after nouns, as in *kitchen in*. So, whereas in English one says *Taro is eating an apple in the kitchen*, in Japanese one says *Taro apple is eating kitchen in*. Transfer of the L1 grammar means that, in advance of receiving Japanese input, English speakers will begin with the assumption that Japanese is also head-initial, an (unconscious) assumption that will later have to be revised.

In terms of processing strategies, L1 transfer involves using L1 strategies to interpret L2 input until they prove inadequate, at which point the learner must adopt new strategies appropriate for the L2. Research on the interpretation of ambiguous sentences provides one of the most clear-cut cases of transfer of L1-specific processing strategies to the L2. Consider the following sentence, in which the complex NP *the servant of the actress* is followed by the ambiguous relative clause (RC) *who was standing on the balcony*:

Someone shot the servant of the actress who was standing on the balcony.

This sentence is ambiguous because the RC could refer to either *the servant* (the first NP) or *the actress* (the second NP). Put differently, either the servant or the actress could have been standing on the balcony. Interestingly, native speakers have preferences for one NP over another, and these preferences are not the same across languages. When asked, "Who was standing on the balcony?" after reading sentences like the one above, English monolinguals usually choose the second NP (the actress). In contrast, when Spanish and French monolinguals read the same sentences in their native language, they usually choose the first NP (the servant). Research in L2 sentence processing shows that L2 learners transfer their L1 preference. That is, Spanish-speaking ESL learners will initially link ambiguous RCs to the first NP, just as they do in their L1. To the extent that English speakers intend to refer to the second NP when they say these types of sentences, Spanish-speaking ESL learners will need to acquire the strategy of linking RCs to the second NP of complex NPs to successfully comprehend the English input.

Reflection

One type of transfer that is less attested in SLA is transfer of morphological inflections. Although you'll occasionally hear an English-speaking learner of Spanish add the English possessive to a Spanish noun (e.g., *Juan's libro* 'John's book'), you'd never hear them add the regular past (*–ed*) or the progressive (*–ing*) morphemes to

Spanish verbs. Likewise, Spanish-speaking ESL learners never add the Spanish inflections associated with grammatical gender marking (–o and –a) to English adjectives. Why do you think this is the case? What is it about inflections that make them more resistant to transfer? (Hint: think about the mental lexicon where inflections are stored. How is it created? How is it organized? What types of problems would bulk transfer of the L1 lexicon cause in L2 learning?)

Many people believe that if the L1 is the starting point for SLA, then it must be the primary cause of errors in the L2. This is a misbelief that has its origins in behaviorism, a dominant theory in psychology during the first half of the 20th century that had profound influence on our initial beliefs about how humans learn language and the role that the L1 plays in L2 learning. Behaviorism posited that all learning in humans and animals was the result of habit formation, which involved making repeated associations between a stimulus and a response. The idea behind behaviorism was that good habits (i.e., desirable responses to stimuli) could be encouraged with rewards. Likewise, bad habits (i.e., undesirable responses to stimuli) could be discouraged via correction. Behaviorists believed that language, like any other human behavior, was a set of habits that could be learned by way of conditioning. That is, correct use of language could be encouraged with rewards, such as positive responses from interlocutors or successful communication, and incorrect use could be corrected. Learning new habits required numerous repetitions of the appropriate stimulus-response association. Once learned, though, a habit was difficult to unlearn and could inhibit future learning. Accordingly, behaviorists believed that one's L1 habits interfered with the learning of new L2 habits where the two differed, and that the L1 was the root cause of all errors in the L2. These beliefs had profound effects on language instruction that are still felt today. In the classroom, errors were to be avoided at all cost, lest they become bad habits, so instruction consisted largely of intensive pattern practice via mechanical (i.e., non-meaning-based) drills and hypercorrection of learner errors.

In reality, L1 influence is much more selective and nuanced than what behaviorism claimed, as the following cases illustrate. In English, object pronouns such as *her* follow conjugated verbs (e.g., *John called her*) but in Spanish they precede them (e.g., *Juan la llama*). English speakers learning Spanish often use SVO order in Spanish sentences that require SOV, which results in errors such as **Juan llama la*. This would appear to be a clear case of L1 transfer, were it not for the fact that Spanish-speaking ESL learners rarely make the equivalent error of producing SOV (**John her calls*) where English requires SVO. This raises the possibility that perhaps SVO is a default that learners resort to in L2 learning, which just so happens to overlap with the order required of English. Similarly, learners make errors that can't be attributed to the L1. Swedish and German, for example, allow SVO word order and adverb fronting (i.e., movement of adverbs to the front of sentences as in *Yesterday he went to Stockholm* vs. *He went to Stockholm yesterday*). When adverbs are fronted, both languages require subject-verb inversion so that the verb is the second word in the sentence, as in *Yesterday went he to Stockholm*. In a study that tested Swedish-speaking learners of L2 German, researchers found that learners produced a word order pattern—adverb fronting without inversion—that is not only ungrammatical in the L2, but also in the L1! This type of evidence suggests that L1 transfer may hinge on developmental readiness. That is, properties from the L1 can transfer to the L2, but instead of being bulk transferred at the beginning of SLA, transfer will occur when learners reach the point in L2 development where the L1 properties can be handled. This view is held by proponents of the speech processing theory described earlier in this module, which claims that speech processing procedures (category procedure, NP procedure, VP procedure, etc.) must be relearned in the L2 and cannot be transferred from the L1. However, once an L2 learner acquires a particular procedure, such as the NP procedure, L1 knowledge related to NPs such as gender or number agreement can kick in. Additional evidence in support of a more limited role for the L1 in SLA comes from developmental stages and acquisition orders, which do not vary as a function of learners' L1.

Thus far we have discussed L1 transfer in the creation of mental representations and the development of processing strategies. The L1 also plays a role in a communication strategy that low-level learners make use of when they attempt to produce language that is beyond their current level of ability. The strategy involves thinking of an utterance in the L1 and then inserting L2 words in place of the L1 words. Consider the following sentence, said to me by a native Spanish speaker after I placed a take-out food order: "In ten minutes is ready your order." On the surface, this utterance appears to be the result of transfer from Spanish, which allows post-verbal placement of the subject NP and use of the present tense for actions occurring in the immediate future (a native English speaker would have said, "Your order will be ready in ten minutes."). However, this sentence is a word-for-word translation of how the sentence would be said in Spanish. The non-native speaker appears to have taken an L1 structure and 'dressed it up' in L2 words. This is not transfer; rather, it's a communication strategy that learners resort to when pushed to produce beyond their current abilities. In any event, although the L1 may be the starting point for SLA, its influence on L2 learning is not nearly as strong as once thought. In the following section, we turn our attention to a different type of factor that might account for some of the variable outcomes of SLA: individual differences in L2 learners themselves.

Individual Differences

Most people have heard of what we might call the "good" language learner. This person may speak multiple languages and seems to 'pick up' new ones quickly. The person may also have a good accent and show facility with spoken language. On the flipside, most people have heard someone lament that he or she is not a good language learner. Given similar learning conditions, are some people just better language learners than others? If so, what characteristics do the good learners possess that make them better learners? These and similar questions are addressed by research in **individual differences**. In this line of research, L2 learners usually complete two assessments: one that measures linguistic ability in the L2 and another that measures a factor that varies from person to person. The two sets of scores are then correlated to see if there's a relationship. In this section, we'll focus on individual differences in two areas: aptitude and motivation.

Aptitude refers to a specific talent or ability to learn languages. The precise components that make up aptitude are the subject of debate, but most aptitude tests assess a learner's ability to do a number of tasks, such as remember unfamiliar sound sequences, infer language patterns, and learn new words via association. Several studies have found positive correlations between aptitude and L2 learning. One recent study tested Spanish-speaking learners of L2 Swedish. In the study, participants were pre-tested to ensure that they passed as native Swedish speakers in ordinary conversation. Those who met the criterion took a Swedish language aptitude test and a grammaticality judgment task that included complex structures known to pose difficulty to L2 learners of Swedish. The results showed that every adult L2 learner who passed for a native speaker in everyday conversation had high verbal aptitude. For these learners, the correlation between aptitude and performance on the grammaticality judgment task was robust (but short of statistical significance). The study also tested adults whose age of onset of SLA occurred in early childhood. Interestingly, the results showed that the vast majority of child starters who performed in the native speaker range on the judgment task also had above-average aptitude. This suggests that high verbal aptitude is required to achieve native-like abilities in the L2 even when SLA begins very early in life.

The results of this study and many others like it are interesting, but it's not clear that they speak to acquisition as we've defined here; that is, as the creation of an implicit linguistic system. First, aptitude tests tend to measure abilities associated with explicit language learning, such as conscious detection of language patterns and associative memory. Aptitude tests were invented during the heyday of behaviorism, a time when classroom language learning consisted of pattern drills and rote memorization, and they haven't changed much since then. Second, most studies assess linguistic ability via tests that tap learners' explicit knowledge of the L2, such as grammaticality judgment tasks. In this light, significant correlations between aptitude and L2 ability are hardly surprising. In contrast, studies that attempt to correlate aptitude with implicit knowledge are rare and the few that exist find no relationship between aptitude and the measurements taken in the study. So, aptitude, as it is currently conceived and measured, may be a good predictor of how L2 learners will perform on certain types of language-related tasks. However, these tasks are not believed to have any bearing on the outcome of acquisition as defined here. What about motivation?

Motivation is a psychological construct that refers to why people decide to do something, how long they are willing to sustain the activity, and how hard they will pursue it. Given that acquisition is slow and takes quite a bit of time, it stands to reason that an L2 learner would need to be highly motivated to stick with language learning long enough to achieve native-like abilities. However, this does not mean that motivation plays a role in *how language is learned*, just as it doesn't play a role in *how* humans lose weight. Someone who is motivated to lose weight will engage in more behaviors conducive to weight loss, such as exercising and eating low-calorie foods, but motivation itself doesn't alter any of the biochemical processes involved in metabolism and calorie burning, which ultimately result in weight loss. Motivation gets you off of the couch and into the gym so that you can engage in those behaviors that do have an impact on weight loss. The same goes for SLA. Highly motivated learners usually get farther than less motivated learners because they engage in more activities that are conducive to acquisition. They seek out more sources of L2 input, such as reading or watching TV in the L2, and make more attempts to interact with native speakers of the L2. None of this changes *how* acquisition happens. Motivated learners still endure all of the pitfalls of L2 comprehension, such as overreliance on lexical items for meaning at the expense of inflections, and must traverse the same hierarchy of processing procedures required of L2 speech production. Motivated learners don't get to skip stages of development, but they may pass through them faster because they get much more of the input required to propel development of the implicit system. One reason that motivation gets so much attention in SLA is that learning an L2 is usually a conscious choice that people make. In contrast, no one chooses to learn an L1. In any event, motivation has more to do with the effort that learners make to spend time on task and less to do with how learning happens. In the following section, we'll touch on the role that instruction plays in adult L2 learning.

Instruction

Everyone who enrolls in a language class or pursues a profession in language teaching does so assuming that instruction makes a difference. To be sure, instruction can mean a variety of endeavors, from playing games in the classroom to drilling students on structures. For the purpose of the present discussion, we are limited to purposeful attempts by instructors and materials to get learners to acquire structural properties of language. This would normally include some kind of explanation plus some kind of focused practice. Instruction is a topic that is covered in much more detail in other modules in this series, but we can address the broader question of whether instruction makes a difference by highlighting what instruction can and cannot do. Classrooms offer a number of advantages over naturalistic language learning environments, so let's start with what instruction can do.

First, the input that classroom language learners get tends to be much more varied and complex than what naturalistic learners get. In addition to spoken input, classrooms provide written input representative of a variety of registers, such as stories, newspapers, essays, and so forth. Second, instruction can help learners become better processors of input by steering them away from inefficient interpretation strategies, such as the lexical preference strategy. More information about the instructional treatment that does this (called Processing Instruction) can be found in the *Suggestions for further reading* at the end of this module. Third, in tutored settings, the communicative demands placed on L2 learners are greatly reduced compared to the world outside the classroom. Teachers modify their speech (e.g., by pausing more often, speaking in shorter sentences, enunciating vowels more clearly, etc.) to make themselves more comprehensible. They may also shoulder more of the burden of communication so that learners do not have to produce beyond their means. For example, teachers may avoid open-ended questions, such as "Where shall we meet?" in favor of questions that demand less spontaneous production from the learner, such as "Where shall we meet, in my office or in the classroom?"

On the flipside, research has been clear in that instruction cannot alter how language develops in the mind/brain over time. Before reaching the stage of using auxiliaries in English negation (stage 4), ESL learners must first go through the stages of placing negators externally (stage 1) and later internally (stage 2). Teaching auxiliaries to learners who are still in stage 1 or 2 will not allow them to jump to stage 4 without having passed through the preceding stages. In a similar way, a parent cannot teach a child to run if they haven't yet gone through the prerequisite steps of standing, learning to balance, and walking. Likewise, in the acquisition of ESL morphemes, instruction cannot force acquisition of morphemes lower in the acquisition order, such as the regular past or the possessive, if morphemes higher in the order have yet to be acquired (e.g., progressive, plural).

Reflection

Given everything you've learned about SLA so far, explain why the verb relay activity described at the beginning of this module is not the type of activity that would further acquisition.

Can L2 Learners Become Native-Like?

Having discussed several factors that might impact acquisition, we are left with a final question: Can L2 learners become native-like? There is evidence that says they can, but there is also evidence that says they can't. This is true regardless of whether the research looks at comprehension or production, and regardless of the particular subcomponent of language that is the focus of the research (e.g., syntax, phonology, morphology). How does one reconcile such conflicting findings? Given the substantial number of studies in which L2 learners perform in native-like ways, it seems fair to say that L2 learners *can* become native-like. However, in the light of many findings that suggest otherwise, it's also fair to say that most *do not* become native-like. Indeed, it's often easy to spot a non-native speaker, particularly as it concerns pronunciation. If this sounds discouraging, keep in mind that at least some of the non-native outcomes found in SLA research are not perceivable outside of the research lab. Many highly proficient L2 learners can pass for native speakers in everyday conversation—as determined by panels of blinded native speaker judges—and yet still show levels of non-nativeness when their linguistic abilities are scrutinized in fine detail, as happens in SLA research. These fine levels of detail matter quite a bit for the advancement of research in the language sciences, but may not matter much to the learner who has attained a high level of proficiency in the L2 and who communicates successfully with native speakers. And that's OK.

Quiz

Take the following short quiz to see what you have learned since the last quiz. Answers are given at the end, so don't peek.

1. The process whereby new forms are added to the learner's implicit linguistic system is called . . .

   a. restructuring.
   b. staged development.
   c. accommodation.
   d. lexical access.

2. Which of the following statements about developmental stages is TRUE?

   a. Some learners can skip stages.
   b. Learners go through stages at roughly the same rate.

    c. Errors of the previous stage cease when a new stage is reached.

    d. none of the above

3. Acquisition orders . . .

    a. refer to how learners acquire one particular form or structure.

    b. vary based on a learner's L1.

    c. are determined by examining learners' accuracy of use.

    d. can be altered with communicative-oriented language instruction.

4. The speech processing procedure that enables L2 learners to produce subject-verb agreement is called the . . .

    a. sentence procedure.

    b. category procedure.

    c. verb phrase procedure.

    d. noun phrase procedure.

5. The critical period refers to a hypothesized window of time during which language learners must . . .

    a. complete their acquisition of language.

    b. get their first exposure to language input.

    c. both (a) and (b).

    d. none of the above

6. Which of the following statements about L1 transfer is FALSE?

    a. It can affect any subcomponent of language.

    b. It can affect how learners process L2 input.

    c. It causes most of the errors that L2 learners make.

    d. more than one of the above

7. Motivation is best described as a measure of a person's . . .

    a. innate ability.

    b. effort.

    c. skill.

    d. outlook on success.

8. A major benefit of instruction is that it can . . .

    a. prevent learners from making errors.

    b. guarantee more native-like outcomes.

    c. get learners to produce beyond their ability.

    d. provide richer and more comprehensible input.

[Answers: 1. c; 2. d; 3. c; 4. a; 5. b; 6. c; 7. b; 8. d]

Summary and Conclusion

In this module, we have covered some of the basic facts about how humans learn L2s in adulthood. We began with the premise that acquisition involves the creation of a mental grammar that exists outside of a learner's conscious awareness. From there, we discussed the types of internal mechanisms that make use of input data and demonstrated that input processing plays a critical role in the type of data that is ultimately delivered to those mechanisms. We saw that development of the implicit system is slow, but also that the system is predisposed to develop in certain ways that cannot be altered by external influences, such as error correction and instruction. Finally, we discussed a number of factors believed to impact L2 learning and showed that most of these factors, as they are currently investigated, speak to the development of something other than an implicit linguistic system (e.g., aptitude), or speak to how much time (e.g., age) or effort (e.g., motivation) one invests in activities conducive to language learning.

The topics covered in this module have a number of implications for contemporary language teaching. First, learners need exposure to input, where input means language that learners must attend to for its meaning. Second, instruction needs to work in tandem with natural processes and not against them. Third, learners cannot be expected to access their implicit systems for production before they've built up mental representations to draw on. Asking learners to produce grammatical structure—even in meaning-oriented output activities—before they've had the opportunity to connect this structure to meaning during comprehension is tantamount to putting the proverbial cart before the horse.

Discussion Questions and Projects

1. Observe a language class and take note of the language that learners get from the instructor, classroom materials, and other students. How much of it constitutes input as we defined it? 100%? 75%? Less than 50%? How much classroom language use is in the learners' L1? 10%? 25%? Greater than 50%?
2. It's common to hear teachers make statements like the following: "The best way to learn a language is to just speak it. That's why I use activities that get learners talking." Explain why this instructor's ideas about language learning and, consequently, language teaching are misguided.
3. Have you ever wondered what language learners think about how languages are learned? Find out by asking a group of students to indicate whether they agree with the following statements—all of which are misconceptions—about L2 learning using a 3-point scale:

Agree, Disagree, No opinion. What do you find? Choose one misconception and offer a suggestion for how teachers could address it in class.

- The best way to learn a language is to just speak it.
- People can learn languages in adulthood and achieve native-like abilities.
- The best predictor of language learning success is motivation.
- If an instructor doesn't correct errors, students will keep making them.
- Some people are just better language learners than others.
- Most of the errors that learners make are caused by interference from the first language.

4. Review the acquisition order for ESL morphemes presented in this module. What are some possible reasons why the progressive (*–ing*) is acquired before the simple past (*–ed*), and why third-person *–s* is the last verbal morpheme to be acquired? (Hint: think about how frequent, salient, and redundant a morpheme is in the input, as well as whether a morpheme is associated with one or multiple meanings and pronunciations.)
5. All learners need exposure to aural input. However, some learners benefit from having written input, too. What types of individual differences do you think underlie why some learners need written input?
6. Do you believe that you have native-like abilities in your L2? Explain your answer. If you rate yourself as nonnative-like in any way, do you believe that you *could* become native-like in that area over time? Why or why not?

Suggested Further Reading

Gass, S. M., Behney, J., & Plonsky, L. (2013). *Second language acquisition: An introductory course*. 4th ed. New York: Routledge.

VanPatten, B. (Ed.). (2004). *Processing instruction: Theory, research, and commentary*. Mahwah, NJ: Erlbaum.

VanPatten, B., & Benati, A. G. (in press). *Key terms in second language acquisition*. 2nd ed. London: Bloomsbury Press.

VanPatten, B., & Williams, J. (Eds.). (2015). *Theories in second language acquisition: An introduction*. 2nd ed. New York: Routledge.

#0173 - 011117 - C0 - 229/152/2 - PB - 9781138500891